C000265038

A BOOT UP

THE RIVER TEIGN

Philip Carter

First published in Great Britain in 2011

British Library Cataloguing-in-Publication Data
A CIP record for this title is available from the British Library

ISBN 978 0 85710 047 4

PiXZ Books
Halsgrove House, Ryelands Business Park,
Bagley Road, Wellington, Somerset TA21 9PZ
Tel: 01823 653777
Fax: 01823 216796
email: sales@halsgrove.com

An imprint of Halstar Ltd, part of the Halsgrove group of companies
Information on all Halsgrove titles is available at: www.halsgrove.com

Printed and bound in China by Toppan Leefung Printing Ltd

Contents

How to use this book

The Area

This is a selection of short walks mostly in and around the River Teign. They are generally circular so that you can easily re-walk them a second time the other way round. Whilst they all have high scenic value they have also been chosen because of items of local interest.

The 'level' shown near the beginning of each walk is an indication of the exertion required. ❤ ❤ ❤ will take more effort than ❤ ❤ and ❤ ❤ more than ❤ .

Some walks pass places of refreshment others do not. But you are always advised to carry a flask and a little something to eat. An empty stomach can mar even the prettiest view!

Go well shod with footwear that has a grip as this will make even the hardest walk easier.

South Devon is a tourist area but many of the walks seek out the quieter corners and you should find them usually pleasantly peaceful.

Eight of the ten walks are on the River Teign. The other two are nearby in the South Devon region.

The River Teign (pronounced 'tin') has an exciting history as varied as the country it flows through, from the high moor to the sea. From iron-age hill forts in the upper valleys, to the 11th century invasion and burning of the village of Teignton (probably Kingsteignton) by the Danes. From Roman bridge foundations found at Teignbridge to recordings in the Domesday Book. From a ferry service at Teignmouth dating back at least to the 13th century to the arrival of the railway line to Teignmouth and Newton Abbot in the 1840s. For the industries of fishing, agriculture, forestry and mining, and the leats and water wheels which helped to run them, the River Teign has continuously supported the various communities along its route. Of its many tributaries the main ones are the Rivers Lemon and Bovey.

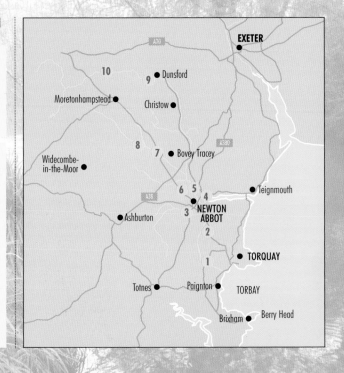

Key to Symbols Used

Level of difficulty:

Easy 🌿

Fair 🌿 🌿

More challenging 🌿 🌿 🌿

Map symbols:

🚗 Park & start

⋯⋯ Road

- - - - Walk

■ Building / Town

+ Church

🍺 Pub

👬 WC

1 Cockington, Torquay

A very easy and pleasant walk close to urban Torquay

Length: 1.5 miles or 2.4 kilometres
Level:
Start: Park at the main Cockington Car Park where there are public toilets 894 638.
Maps: OS Map Explorer 110 Torquay & Dawlish.
Refreshments: there are several cafes in the village, plus Cockington Court and the Drum Inn spoil you for choice.

Cockington has a long history, being mentioned in the Domesday Book. Two centuries on Sir Roger de Cockington was one of Devon's parliamentary representatives in 1258.

Some four centuries later Sir Henry Carey of Cockington was impoverished by being heavily fined after the Civil War for his support of the Royalist cause. This enabled the Mallocks, a family of Exeter merchants, to purchase Cockington in 1654.

Yet Cockington's recent story is more intriguing; Torquay expanded fast as a resort and the local landowners grew rich in the process. The Mallocks however eschewed a fortune by not allowing development. Then as late as the 1930s

there was a change of mind and a Trust was formed, a tasteful model community was to be permitted and Lutyens was asked to plan it. Work actually started but then came to a halt. Happily the centre of the old village was largely untouched.

Wooden Boardwalk
Mill Pond
Water Wheel
ose Garden
Cockington Forge
1
7
ockington rish Church
5
Cockington
Lower Lodge
Gamekeeper's Cottage
3
2
4
Manscombe Plantation

The Lower Lodge at Cockington

(1) Leave the car park by the entrance turning left. Almost immediately you reach a crossroads turn neither left nor right but go ahead with the old forge on your right.

The old forge is now just a much photographed visual attraction but well within living memory it had a blacksmith who shod horses.

Cockington Forge

Proceed along valley ignoring public footpath to 'Seafront' on left and later public bridleway on right.

(2) Shortly turn right in driveway entrance signposted 'The Lakes, Game Keeper's Cottage and Woodland Walks'. This is the old Lower Lodge of Cockington Court and you go up under the arch.

Walking under the Rhododendrons at Cockington

Cockington, Torquay

(3) When you reach the first lake swing very sharply left keeping the lake on your right. As you ascend keep beside lake ignoring path going left named 'Woodland Walk'.

At the end of the first lake go ahead beside a second lake, ignoring paths left and right. Proceed from second to third lake up the steps again ignoring paths left and right.

(4) At the Game keeper's Cottage under Manscombe Woods swing right and at the next two path junctions bear left. The second is signposted 'To Cockington

Gunnera, commonly known as giant rhubarb

Village & Court' and the pathway goes under an arch.

(5) At the old stone cider press go left again to join the main driveway, an avenue of trees leading to the main house. Note Cockington Church on your

The Gamekeeper's Cottage

The old church of red sandstone has a most attractive setting much appreciated by wedding photographers. Cockington Court has been altered and extended over the years but most of what you see now dates from the 16th and 17th centuries. Agatha Christie was a guest here participating in amateur dramatics. During World War II the house provided a safe haven for an art collection.

left then walk up between the Court and the Church either up the steps or slightly further from the wall up a tarmac path.

The old granite cider press

Cockington Church of St George & St Mary

Entrance to the
Cockington Rose
Garden in winter

*The Drum Inn which was
originally to be called The
Forge, was the only part
of the planned model
village that was actually
constructed. Even then its
clock, with drum beats
instead of chimes to mark
the time, was never installed.*

6 Look for the narrow entrance to the Rose Garden on your right, a riot of colour in summer. Then return to the front of the Court. Here, possibly refreshed, turn your back to the building and go down the grass valley, close to the cricket pitch. Admittedly when a match is in progress you will be wise to take a more circuitous route!

7 Some way below the pitch take the boardwalk or raised wooden footpath to exit the ground. Enter the Drum Inn gardens through a kissing gate. Turn sharp right to go up steps and left at the top.

Here you walk along the side of the old millpond. At the end of the pond go down the steps to the water wheel at the bottom.

8 Follow down the gravel path through a gap in the wall to a thatched gate leading into the road. Here turn left for the short distance to the car park.

*The old waterwheel that
powered the local mill has
sadly been neglected of late;
it used to turn slowly. It was
made by Beare's of Newton
Abbot (note the maker's
plate), who were at one
time specialist water
wheel manufacturers.*

2 **Kingskerswell**

A rural ramble overlooking a town and village

1 Leave the church car park with its fine horse chestnut trees, to return to the road turning left and shortly forking right uphill, passing Tudor Cottage on your right.

2 At the top you learn you have come up Church End Road. Now turn left down Greenhill Road and take Church Lane Way, the unnamed lane on right.

Length: 2.3 miles or 3.7 kilometres
Level: 🥾 🥾
Start: Park at the car park opposite the parish church of St Mary Kingskerswell 876 678
Maps: OS Map Explorer 110 Torquay & Dawlish
Refreshments: none on the walked circuit.

Ruined manor house

Maddacombe Road

Kerswell Down Hill

Whigborough Common

Entry to wood

Greenhill Road

Kingskerswell

The horse chestnut, source of 'conkers', seems a very English sort of tree. In fact it is not indigenous and only arrived from the Balkans in the sixteenth century. In spring its candle-like flowers make a most attractive sight.

13

St. Mary's Church at the start of the walk

There is no direction sign but there is a notice 'Unsuitable for motor vehicles'. This is part of the John Musgrave Heritage Trail. The tarmac soon ceases.

There are footpaths off left then right but keep with the track. You pass an assortment of gates. A big barn comes into sight ahead and there is a right turn signed 'Public Footpath'.

 Take this stony route continuing uphill.

The path becomes narrower and is eventually blocked with a wooden rail fence and you cross the stile into the wood. Presently there is a left fork 'Public Footpath'; do not take it but go ahead on the unsigned path. Watch out for spindle trees.

The spindle tree is usually small and insignificant, growing in dense woodland. However in autumn its vivid yellow seeds in their pink casing attract the eye. So named because it was once used to make spindles for spinning woollen thread, the wood was also used to make knitting needles in pre-plastic days when knitting was commonplace.

The amazing colours of the spindle tree

Distant view of the one-time St Augustine's Priory

(4) The wood ends and becomes the open Whigborough Common. Bear left keeping outside the wood to come to a view point overlooking Stoneycombe Quarry.

The part of the name 'Kings' tell us it was once a royal estate and 'Kerswell' that watercress grew here, and in fact it still does.

Stoneycombe Quarry

Stoneycombe Quarry is somewhat like 'topsy', it started relatively small and has grown and grown. The larger quarry has meant diverting footpaths and it even at one stage swallowed a pleasant old house to improve its car parking facilities. It has in fact been worked for over 150 years under a series of ownerships. It has kept steadily busy but particularly so with the improvements to the road into Exeter at Telegraph Hill and the Scott and Lawes Bridges at the entry to Torquay.

When you've looked turn right, but here is the clever bit: there are two exits from the common, one near the scarp the other a few yards further 'inland' away from steep incline. If you take this 'inland' route you will get a somewhat easier passage through the woods.

(5) Go through the stone gateway at the start of this sinuous route. There are minor paths leading off but stay with the main path. At the one major junction fork left.

Later another main track comes in from the right but bear left ahead. There is a brief open space then back into the wood.

6 Eventually you come to another viewpoint with a metal seat. A good spot for coffee if you brought some. Look left for Abbotskerswell and Dartmoor in the distance, centrally for the former St Augustine's Priory and Wolborough Hill, Newton Abbot. In the foreground is the main Newton Abbot to Plymouth railway line.

St Augustine's Priory

St Augustine's Priory was originally a private estate named Abbotsleigh, but was purchased for the use of a Roman Catholic religious order in 1863. The sisters arrived from Spettisbury in Dorset some fifty strong by special train, but by 1983 the numbers had dwindled to two and they left by car. The priory buildings were converted into flats and maisonettes in 1986, but the evocative graveyard where the sisters were buried remains.

7 The wood opens a little. You pass a wooden pole above a small industrial complex. There are then a series of downhill grassy paths to cross Kingskerswell Downs, the middle one is to be preferred but they eventually all join.

8 There is a metal handrail down the steepest part and you come out to the road.

Take care as here the road can be busy at times. Turn right, this is Maddacombe Road, at the junction turn left and very shortly turn right at an acute angle to go down a quieter lane.

9 At the bottom of the lane turn left and then bear left to get back to the car park.

(Short extension, if ruins interest you. Do not go into car park but continue along the road. Just past a second gate into the church is a pedestrian wooden gate into the graveyard. Go through this to turn left up a grassy young beech avenue to get to the ruins of Kingskerswell Manor House. Then retrace your steps to the car park).

Kingskerswell beyond the bell tower of St Mary's Church

Kingskerswell Manor House

The substantial fortified Kingskerswell Manor House was owned by several families over the years, the Dinhams (one of whom in the fifteenth century was Chancellor of England), de Moeles and Courtenay. Like so many houses of this type it was often enlarged and improved. The oldest parts date back at least to the thirteenth century and its greatest days seem to have been in the sixteenth century. It was abandoned by the middle of the nine-teenth century and then seems to have been largely and perhaps surprisingly forgotten until a recent upsurge in interest.

The ruins of Kingskerswell Manor House

St Mary's Church

If you have the time the church is worth a visit. It dates back to at least the fourteenth century and was once the private chapel of the Manor House. There are effigies of the Dinhams on the north window ledges.

3 Bradley Woods, Newton Abbot

An old favourite of the author's. Generally a very easy walk but there is a rough stretch at the start of the descent from the highest point of the walk.

Length: 2.5 miles or 4 kilometres
Level: 🥾 🥾
Start: Park in the car park on the edge of Baker's Park, Newton Abbot at the bottom of Stepps Meadow 853 709
Maps: OS Map Explorer 110 Torquay & Dawlish
Refreshments: none on the walking circuit, plenty in Newton Abbot.

1 Walk back to where car park widens to turn left over a concrete bridge. Very shortly there is a footpath turning right which ignore. Proceed ahead to T junction on a track, turn left again to follow along the side of the leat.

Ignore another path on right, passing through a gate to walk for short while along the bank of River Lemon on your left and the leat on your right.

2 When you reach a stone weir on your right go with the right fork of the path leaving the river.

The River Lemon is a short river, rising below Haytor on the edge of Dartmoor, but because of its considerable fall in a short distance is swiftly flowing. This river was an ideal source of waterpower for a series of mills ranging from the

Bridge over the River Lemon, Bradley Woods

21

Elderberry in blossom behind the stone wall at Bradley Manor

usual corn mills, to a less common edge-tool mill and an even rarer bark mill for the local tannery. The name Lemon probably derives from the Celtic 'abounding in elms' although several other origins have been suggested.

Go forward past a stone bridge on your right which crosses the leat to join a metalled drive turning neither right nor left.

 The drive leads you past the main gate of Bradley Manor, it

Leat gate off the River Lemon

ceases to be metalled. The way passes several seats, curves right and eventually enters a wood.

Crossing the leat on a stone bridge you come to another weir on the left, go through a gate to enter a field and again walk along close to the river.

4 At the end of the field go through a kissing gate. Turn neither left nor right but go ahead through a second kissing gate. Almost immediately turn left across a railed concrete bridge, passing the site of the one time Ogwell Mill.

Ogwell Mill was a water powered corn mill consisting of three floors and fitted with two pairs of stones driven by an overshot wheel. The mill probably

Weir in the woods

worked until about 1909 and then became popular for cream teas. The mill was an attractive old building and its picture was used as a trademark for a local perfume manufacturer's 'Bradley Woods Bouquet'. They claimed that 'no expense had been spared in its production and that the whole world had been ransacked for precious and costly odours'!

The Puritan Pit is so called because it was used for religious observance in less tolerant times. William Yeo, the Church of England curate of Wolborough, because of his strong beliefs, was in 1662 ejected from his living and had at times to leave his home and even preach in Bradley Woods at night. It is sometimes called Preacher's Pit or more illogically- Devil's Pit! Maybe we should not be too sympathetic for William, he would patrol the town together with a constable armed with a stout stick to prevent 'any profanation of the Sabbath' and was a 'terror to loose persons'.

The pungent Ransomes of wild garlic in Bradley Woods

5 Having crossed the bridge shortly swing left again at signedPublic Footpath to go up a slope. Go forward through a waymarked wooden kissing gate.

Go steadily uphill until you reach fenced pit, The Puritan Pit. Keep to the right of it and go ahead.

Stile on the path after the Puritan Pit

Butcher's Broom is a is a dark green spiky woodland shrub that has red berries. It is so called because in days gone by before 'health and safety' ideas it was used by butchers to brush meat scraps off their wooden chopping blocks. One of its alternative names is Knee Holly, for obvious reasons. It is known to flower arrangers as Ruscus.

Cows in the meadow near the former mill site, Bradley Woods

6 Cross a stile and then after a short uphill flight of steps go steeply downhill - at first rough, then stepped. At one point the path swings left and then right. Butcher's broom is often found growing here.

Towards the bottom keep left at footpath junction. Presently you come to another railed concrete bridge on your left but do not cross it, instead go ahead along right river bank.

7 Ignore the footpath going right just as you leave wood and enter a small field. Bear left. At the end of the field leave by a wooden kissing gate and plank bridge.

Go ahead crossing Bradley Manor Drive, turning neither left nor right, to pass a rail fence into the playing field area. Follow the track along the left hand side back to car park.

4 **Hackney, Kingsteignton**

An interesting little walk though admittedly the middle part good, the two ends even better!

(1) Start the walk at the back of the car park, opposite the entrance. Swing right past a five barred gate and very shortly fork left. Later ignore a bridge on left to continue forward. At path crossroads go straight ahead ignoring paths right and left

Rushes are sometimes locally known as windle-straw. The marshy field is a good place to find the showy Yellow Flag Iris. This is also called Sword Flag because of its sharp pointed leaves.

Length: 2.5 miles or 4 kilometres
Level:
Start: Park at Hackney Marshes Nature Reserve Car Park off Greenhill Way, Kingsteignton 872 726
Maps: OS Map Explorer 110 Torquay & Dawlish
Refreshments: both nearby cafés are currently closed but there is a hotel and pub part way round.

where there is a second bridge. At the third bridge turn left to cross the stream. In a few yards when you

reach a fence swing left on to a grassy ill-defined path. At the end of the rushes, bear slightly right along the edge of the field. At the end of the field bear left on a more defined path by a rail fence, the path then goes up a small hill.

Hackney Lane

Hackney Marshes Nature Reserve

Hackney Canal

Hackney

Passage House Inn

Bargees Village Cottages

A380

Yellow flags or sword lily

2 Shortly ignore path on left at top of the rise by T junction to road, bear at first right and then left. When you reach tarmac veer right down past houses. At the road go right again past entrance of River Close to proceed uphill under a road bridge. Ignore public footpath going left to continue up the road to cross railway bridge and go down other side. At the bottom avoid car park on the left to go forward on signed public footpath between grass lawn and the

'Passage' means ferry and long ago there used to be a ferry from this point across the Teign to Netherton on the southern bank. Keep a watch out for little egrets, a small white heron which has long white feathers on the back of its head. They only arrived in England in quantity in the 1980s and started breeding in this country in the 1990s, but are now commonly seen.

Part of the bargees' village beneath the viaduct

Passage House Inn. Turn right along the water side.

3 Pass under a viaduct to come alongside several ruined cottages. Keep going forward along the bank to pass under a gloomy railway arch.

The cottages were once part of a bargees' village; here lived the men

Autumnal view down the Teign estuary

Looking upstream to the railway bridge

who shipped the Kingsteignton area ball-clay down to Teignmouth. It was quite a vibrant community and even had an annual regatta. Surprisingly though, there was no fresh water supply, it too had to be brought in by boat!

④ On leaving the railway fork left. Soon you can turn left to get a better look at what was once the Hackney Canal.

Cross the metal bridge to walk along-side the race course There are views of Newton Abbot and more distantly of

Dartmoor. Cross at the next bridge and swing left to reach the car park.

Ball-clay was originally carried by packhorses to the Teign and then taken down river by boat. Then the Templer family constructed the Stover Canal. Lord Clifford of Chudleigh who still brought his clay by land, was not able to compete with the clay coming down the Stover Canal. He therefore constructed his own Hackney Canal from Kingsteignton which was opened in 1843 and closed in 1930. A vestige of the old canal can still be seen.

5 **Teignbridge along the River Teign**

Deservedly popular and easy canal-side walk

Length: 2.2 miles or 3.5 kilometres
Level: 🥾
Start: Park at the car park close to Teignbridge 858 734
Map: OS Map Explorer 110 Torquay & Dawlish
Refreshments: none on the walked circuit.

(1) Walk back along the road towards Newton Abbot, you can use the grass verge for part of this short stretch. Just before the road bridge over the old canal turn right on a footpath signed 'Templer Way Stover Country park 2 ½ miles'. The narrower track closer to the canal is the better route.

The Stover Canal was built by the Templer family and opened in 1792 to carry their ball-clay. It continued in use for nearly 250 years. It is called 'ball' because when hewn by hand it was cut out in roughly circular lumps. It is in fact china clay with a vegetable matter content. On the North side of the canal bridge is a goat's

Goat's head on the Stover Canal near Teignbridge

Teignbridge along the River Teign

31

Teignbridge along the River Teign

Along the boardwalk

Ball Clay - an explanation

It is quite easy to describe why ball clay is called by that name. It is a far more complicated subject to describe the merits and special properties of the not over-plentiful material. For a start ball clay is only found in three places in the United Kingdom; these are South Devon, North Devon and Dorset, all of which in past geological eras moved away from the high mass of land corresponding to modern Dartmoor. Laid down as sedimentary deposits by huge rivers, ball clay has qualities not found in the china clay mined from deposits such as those found in Cornwall. It is these qualities that make ball clay a much sought after raw material. In fact over 90% is exported. It is principally used in paper, ceramics, sanitary ware, tiles, tableware, plastics and even in medicines.

head. This may have been chosen because Gappah, a local settlement, means 'Goat's Path' and there was track way here running to it.

2 Shortly there is a wooden plank bridge and a stile. Presently the path opens to the right to reveal fields. Alder trees grow alongside the old canal and if you

Meadow flowers near the River Teign

The gas pipeline took gas from the Newton Gasworks to Teigngrace Station for illumination purposes.

look carefully you will see evidence of a gas pipeline. You come to a longish wooden plank bridge followed by a very small one.

 3 The next item of interest is the Graving Dock Lock.

Wildflowers along the canal path

The Graving Dock Lock was used for building and repairing the barges for use on the canal. There was a boiler to raise steam to help shape the wooden planks.

Graving Dock Lock

You proceed forward to a kissing gate to arrive in an open field. Note a large block of abandoned granite.

 4 Here there is a right turn which you want signed

Path junction on the Teignbridge walk with abandoned granite block

'Templer Way Heritage Trail Stover via Ventiford 2½ miles. The small village behind the trees to the west is Teigngrace.

(5) (Optional short extension, if canals interest you: do not turn right but walk straight ahead signed 'Templer Way Heritage Trail Stover via Lock's Bridge 2 miles'. In a few yards there is an information panel on left hand side. Then there is a sign pointing left across a bridge and an unsigned path going forward. Take this unsigned path and look left to see the old lock. Having looked retrace your steps but this time of course take a left turn across the field via the concrete bridge.)

Go across concrete bridge to take a track across the field. At the end of the field there is a wooden plank bridge and a kissing gate to enter a second field. The way is no longer a track but a grass path.

 At the end of the second field there is another kissing gate.

The River Teign's name comes from a Celtic derivation meaning 'the sweeper'.

The settlement of Teigngrace takes is name from the river and from the 'Gras' family who lived here in the fourteenth century.

Pass through and go to the bank of the River Teign where you turn right at a waymarked post.

 The rest of the way is all along the river bank. Soon you pass into a second field and then a third with a less defined boundary. There is then one last field (note the plantains under your feet), before the road. The path veers right to get to a gate into the road. Cross with care to regain car park.

Plantains are able to survive the hard wear of a well-used path better than most plants, this is because new growth takes place at the base of the plant.

Walking towards the Teign River from the Stover Canal

6 **Stover Lake near Drum Bridges**

An easy walk entirely within the Stover Country Park

① Walk down past the Visitor Centre signed 'To Templer Way.' At the path junction swing right and then bear left, there is a further sign but a bit out of the way, 'Templer Way Heritage Trail Teignmouth, to reach the lake.

Stover Lake is not natural but is an artificial pool. It was constructed as part of the landscaping for the Templers' vast estate which stretched up to and included Haytor. Three generations of the family lived at Stover House: James Senior, James Junior and grandson George. Afterwards it was sold to the Duke of Somerset and is now a school.

② Here go left to cross a bridge then walk along with the lake beside you on your

Length: 2.3 miles or 3.7 kilometres
Level: 🥾
Start: Park in the car park at Stover Country Park close to Visitor Centre 832 749
Maps: OS Map Explorer 110 Torquay & Dawlish
Refreshments: a snack-wagon/ice cream van is sometimes in the car park area.

right. Keep beside the lake on the right hand side crossing a second bridge. Path going left signed 'Children's Trail' ignore. Ignore second path on left signposted 'To Arboretum'. Cross a short plank bridge over a ditch. Pass a notice on 'Pond Life'.

Stover Country Park

Canal

Stover Lake

Visitor Centre

Bird Hide

Overhead Walkway

37

Ducklings adrift at Stover Lake

3. At the end of the lake there is a crossroads, do not turn left or right over the bridge but go ahead to walk along the bank of the canal. At the end of the canal by the water overspill turn sharp right to cross a wooden plank bridge and ascend steps to walk back along the other side of the canal. When you reach the end of the canal, swing left and take the right fork alongside the lake. A little way along turn left on the wooden Aerial Walkway, a high level

One of the whimsical carvings on the Stover Walkway

Bird hide seen from across the lake

Grey squirrels to many are attractive but the older generations will remember with regret the native red squirrels that were driven out from here. Grey squirrels came from North America in the mid 19th century and have now spread nearly everywhere. However, two places that the reds can still be seen in Southern England are Brownsea Island in Poole Harbour and the Isle of Wight.

boarded walk which will bring you back to the lake.

At the turning point look for bird feeders in the trees and for grey squirrels

scavenging fallen seeds on the ground below. On regaining lake turn left.

 At the corner of the lake cross either of the wooden

One of the more attractive birds often seen on the lake is the great crested grebe. In some years several pairs have nested here. They have an elaborate courtship dance and the parents will swim carrying their striped youngsters on their backs.

boardwalks over the water and turn right. Presently there is a lakeside bird hide on the right you may care to visit.

Rhododendrons at Stover Lake

5 At the path junction a little further on turn left to leave the lake and get back to the car park.

7 **Bovey Tracey**

A one time railway route with a river return.

1 Go ahead a few yards to pass through a wooden gate, passing a National Trust omega sign 'Parke Estate.'

The path swings right and goes up a

The Parke Estate was donated to the National Trust by Major William Hole in 1974 and is now the home of the Dartmoor National Park offices. There were earlier houses on the site but the present one dates from early 1800s.

slope to the bed of the old railway line from Bovey Tracey. Early on you cross the River Bovey on a bridge. From then on for the first half of the walk follow its

Length: 2.3 miles or 3.7 kilometres
Level:
Start: Park alongside the left verge of the A382 Bovey Tracey to Moretonhampstead main road just before Hole Bridge 811 785.
Maps: OS Map Explorer 110 Torquay & Dawlish
Refreshments: none actually on the walk but Bovey Tracey is not far away.

RIVER BOVEY

HOLE BRIDGE

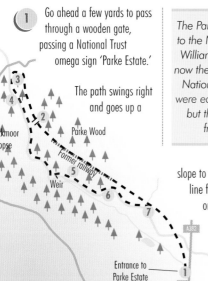

Blackmoor Copse

Parke Wood

Former railway

Weir

A382

Entrance to Parke Estate

Gate leading down to the river at Parke

The Newton Abbot to Moretonhampstead railway line opened for passenger traffic in 1866 running through Bovey Tracey and Lustleigh. It closed in 1958 after nearly a hundred years in use. It was nicknamed the 'Moreton Flier' though in truth it was anything but that! Stories abound of the friendly unhurried way in which it was operated.

course, the route is always obvious and perhaps unexpectedly attractive. There are various footpath cross-roads and side paths but railways rarely turn at right angles or use fierce slopes so just keep going ahead. Sometimes on little embankments sometimes in old cuttings.

2 An overhead arch alerts you to the fact you are approaching your turn off point. At the next footpath junction after the arch there is another National Trust omega sign 'Parke Estate' turn left here down a slope.

3 At the bottom of the slope fork left. There are a couple of small paths leading off but

The Parke Weir, built to supply the leat

Mist rising over the river at Parke

follow the main walked route to the River Bovey where you turn left.

(4) Presently you pass a wooden bridge spanning the river but do not use it, stay on the same side. Later the path leaves the bank for a short while but continue in the same direction to regain the river and pass through two kissing gates. In places there are several alternative paths but as long as you follow the river along you will not get lost.

(5) There is a plank bridge crossing a ditch. Presently the path opens out with a small meadow along one side. Cross a boardwalk, turn right to continue with the river through an open meadow.

The cliff path on the return

The River Bovey is a tributary of the Teign. It rises on Dartmoor and joins the Teign at a quiet spot north of Ventiford, the terminus of the one time Stover Canal.

6 Cross a plank bridge and then go steeply up steps. An attractive little stretch but you need to take care where you are putting your feet. Cross a stile to enter a field continuing with the river.

7 At the end of the field go up steps again to rejoin the old railway line. Here turn right to go back the short distance to where you parked your car.

Walkers and cyclists on the track bed of the former railway

8 **Hisley Bridge, Lustleigh Cleave**

A woodland walk using an old pack-horse bridge.

(1) Go through the gate at the top end of the car park signed 'Permissive Bridleway to Old Manaton Road'. There are some minor paths leading off but stay with the main track.

(2) The way goes steadily uphill the steepest stretch being near the top. Go through a gate and then a very few yards further to turn right on the old road, noting the holly in the hedgerow.

(3) The way is now down hill and you cross a stream. The route levels out and just after a substantial boulder on the right swing right and go through a gate marked 'Hisley Wood'. There is a sign too but it

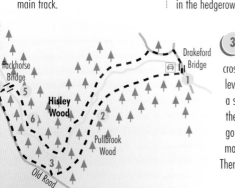

Drakeford Bridge

Packhorse Bridge

Hisley Wood

Pullbrook Wood

Old Road

Length: 2 miles or 3.2 kilometres
Level: ♥
Start: Park at the car park for Pullbrook Wood near Drakeford Bridge 789 801
Maps: OS Map Explorer OL28 Dartmoor.
Refreshments: The Cleave Inn, Lustleigh is nearby

Cleave according to the Oxford English Dictionary means a 'cleft'. In the South West it is used for steep, often wooded river valleys, hence Lustleigh, Belstone, Tavy Cleaves etc.

The holly traditionally used for Christmas decoration grows nearly everywhere save for damp ground. Although not a tall tree it is sometimes prominent in old hedgerows because of a superstition that it was unlucky to cut it so that it was often left to outgrow its near neighbours. People are surprised to see some trees with an abundance of berries whilst other trees nearby have none. The reason for this in a that there are male and female forms of the tree and only the latter bear fruit.

Holly berries along the old Manaton Road

is not well situated so you may miss it. 'Public Bridlepath Rudge and Ford footpath Lustleigh Cleave or Pack Saddle Bridge'

4 After going through the gate fork right to get to the old pack horse bridge. A pleasant spot to stop and look around especially if you have brought a flask!

5 Having crossed the bridge swing sharp right to take the path downstream along the River Bovey. Signed 'Public Footpath Lustleigh Road near Packsaddle Bridge'.

6 Shortly pass through a pedestrian gate; here the woodland thins.

Hisley packhorse bridge

7 Presently go through a further gate into a field, signed 'Public Footpath'. After a while the grass path swings left away from the river to come to a gate into the road,

8 Turn right and at the road junction turn right again to cross Drakeford Bridge, look south to see Pullabrook Farm and take a last turn right back into the car park.

It seems unlikely but Pullabrook once had a railway station! It began as Hawkmoor Halt named after the sanatorium a couple of miles away up a steep hill. The old joke was that it thinned the patient intake because few survived the climb! Maybe due to

The dark green round-leaved alder tree likes a moist situation in which to grow. Once it had a considerable commercial value, the wood being used to make clogs much in demand in industrial areas. In the summertime parties of workmen would descend from Lancashire on such places as Lustleigh to camp, on what is now the cricket field, and harvest the wood. They were a rough lot and the locals were well advised to lock up their daughters!

criticism, it was decided to rename the station and it became Pullabrook. However, the Moretonhamstead line closed in 1955 so it only had four years use with that new name.

Looking back at Hisley Bridge

9 Steps Bridge near Dunsford

If you can, try this one in spring when the wild daffodils are at their best, but it is always a lovely walk.

Dunsford

In times gone by, towns were often known for specific items made there. For instance Redditch in Worcestershire for needles and Witney in Oxfordshire for blankets. Dunsford near by was known for its production of edge-tools especially by the Morris Brothers. Their great staple was billhooks, essential tools in the days of miles of hedgerows and no modern tractor hedge-trimmers. They also made garden implements. Morris Brothers were well known throughout Devon as the 'Rolls Royce' of tool makers.

This walk looks superficial as a there-and-back rather than the more usual circular route. However, by using the three loop paths one way and coming back the other, only a little of the way need be walked

Length: 3.5 miles or 5.6 kilometres.
Level: 🐾
Start: Park at the car park next to the Steps Bridge Hotel on the B3212 road 803 883. There are also a few roadside parking spaces close to the beginning of the footpath but they are often full.
Maps: OS Map Explorer 110 Torquay & Dawlish
Refreshments: not on the walk route

twice. The suggestion is to take the signed right fork each time and then on the return stay with the river all the way. On the other hand if you wish you can simply walk by the river both ways.

Dunsford Wood

Cod Wood

4

3

2 Weir

Steps Bridge

1

Bridford Wood

51

Gorse

It has alternative names of furze and whin. Most folk seeing yellow gorse today hardly give it a second glance unless it is to avoid getting prickled by it! On this walk there are more spectacular things to look at.

However, once it was more appreciated for its usefulness. It was actually planted to make shelter belts for keeping animals. A practice that has survived on some of the windy Falkland Islands in the South Atlantic until this very day. It also served the domestic purpose of acting as a clothes line for drying, items stuck fast and did not blow away in the wind. It was however as a fuel that it was most extensively used because it burns fiercely. It fired the early enclosed ovens. The method seems strange now, but the gorse was put into the empty oven and burnt there. The ash and debris was raked out as best as could be, then the food, bread etc. to be cooked was put in the hot oven, being sealed again. No fine micro-wave timing then, it was leave it for a while and hope! Needless to say you did not need a charcoal supplement when eating food cooked that way.

Gorse has a place in flower folk-lore. This is because there are two common species that flower at different times of the year. Common gorse flowers a little in late autumn and through the winter, coming into flower most strongly in spring. Western gorse and dwarf furze flower in late summer. Between the different species, some gorse is almost always in flower, hence the old country phrase: "When gorse is out of bloom, kissing's out of fashion".

① From the car park walk down the road towards Exeter to cross River Teign by the road bridge. In a very few yards on the left is the

The daffodils that grow in profusion around Steps Bridge are smaller than their cultivated 'cousins'. They make up one of the great wildflower spectacles. They are not as common through-out the country, but where conditions suit them they always make a brave sight.

Steps Bridge in the snow

Weir at Steps Bridge where the
leat once led off to Dunsford

path you want signed 'Public Bridleway' with a nearby information board 'Dunsford Wood'. Very shortly you pass a small weir. In the right season the area is bright with daffodils.

 2 Soon you come to the first junction signed 'Public Bridlepath' fork right. This area abounds in holly and ferns. There are small paths leading off but main track is obvious.

3 You regain the river at a National Trust omega sign for Dunsford Wood. Later again you have the opportunity of leaving

Path along the river at Steps ridge

the river. And this option is repeated later.

(4) Right towards the end of the path a little meadow opens up between the woodland path and the river with bracken and bluebells in season. You cross a small stream to come to Boyland Road. The sign

THE NATIONAL TRUST

DUNSFORD WOOD

points back to 'Steps Bridge'. Here it is about-turn and as suggested you can walk back all along the riverside for the whole way. The first part is more open meadowland with some old apple trees which may have been planted by the charcoal burners who worked these woods in days gone by.

Coppicing is an ancient form of woodland management still practised in a very few places today. Depending on the use required, trees were rotationally felled but always in blocks leaving another block for processing in several years time. This way the woodsmen never ran out of work, and felling could be a continuing process. Cutting for many uses was at five year intervals but this varied according to variety of tree and uses required of it. One of the common end products was bark for tanning, the wood often being used for charcoal. Smaller material was cut for hurdle and fence making. A surprising use of coppicing was the production of the tall poles for growing hops, the bark of the smaller wood being used for tanning. Hazel and ash were two woods commonly coppiced but a number of other varieties were also grown for the process. Interestingly NT Castle Drogo intend to start coppicing again for their own purposes.

10 Teign Gorge near Drewsteignton

Justifiably one of Devon's classic walks.

Walk down and cross Fingle Bridge. You then have two options. The first turn immediately right beside the river crossing a small granite bridge followed by a small wooden bridge, both over ditches to join the main track. The second is to go a few yards further and turn right directly on to the track at the

National Trust sign for 'Charles & Hannicombe Woods.' The first is the more scenic option.

Just over the top of a rise is a vestige of a track leading left but stay on the main track going along by the river.

2 Much later a forestry track goes off at an acute angle to the left but again stay with the main track.

3 Eventually you come to a fork at the bottom

Length: 4 miles or 6.4 kilometres
Level: 🐾 🐾 🐾
Start: Park beside the road just before Fingle Bridge 743 900.
Maps: OS Map Explorer OL28 Dartmoor
Refreshments: The Fingle Bridge Inn but nowhere else on the circuit unless you divert to the wonderful cafeteria at Castle Drogo although naturally this will add to the distance.

The Fingle Bridge Inn

Map

Castle Drogo
9
Sharp Tor
10
11
Hunter's Tor
4 **3**
5
Old generating turbines
High wall crossing
Whidden Wood
2
Hannicombe Wood
Don't miss the junction!
12
Drewston Wood
Fingle Bridge
1
Weir

Teign Gorge near Drewsteignton

Autumn colours on the River Teign

There used to be a corn mill a little below Fingle Bridge that added to its income by serving refreshments. Unfortunately there was a fire in 1894 which brought milling to an end. Refreshments continued to be served from at first temporary accommodation. Over the years the refreshment hut flourished becoming the The Angler's Rest and is today The Fingle Bridge Inn.

of a slope and again there are two options. The first keep left on the main track, this is the easier route but does involve a bit more climbing. The second is to fork right and at the next

junction go left of the metal roofed building. The path gets narrower and rougher passing the interesting remains of Castle Drogo's electricity generating turbines.

(4) Which ever way you went you come to a big wooden gate which you need to go through. You then walk along by a wall about 8-9

The turbines were built to supply Castle Drogo with hydro-electric power. They operated from 1927 to 1994.

feet high made of massive blocks of granite which was built around 1570 to enclose Sir John Whiddon's fallow deer park.

The latest suspension bridge rebuilt after flooding

The Whortleberry as it is commonly known in the West Country, grows hereabouts but has a number of alternative names, blueberries, blaeberries, win berries even shortened to 'urts' in old Devonshire dialect. It should not be confused with the more recently known 'blueberry' grown for American type muffins. It is a green-leaved shrubby little plant that will grow in poor moorland acidic soil. When the little fruits form they turn from green to red and then to dark blue when ripe. It takes a long time to pick a quantity. In fact some pickers have a spiked open ended type miniature rake to sweep/shovel them up. They taste woody on their own but a little apple ameliorates the flavour. They can be made into jam or put in a pie They came into their own during the Second Word War when fruit was at a premium.

(5) Just before the track leaves the wall there is a sign pointing right 'Castle Drogo and Fingle Bridge'. You need to cross the wall here going steeply down to cross a suspension bridge.

The bridge has had to be replaced twice in recent years. It allows one to cross the Drogo weir. The weir was specially constructed to provide a steady supply of water to the generating turbines. It is an attractive feature at any time and is a superb viewing point for watching salmon return up the River Teign to spawn.

(6) At the other side go up the steps turning left at the top, to at once, fork right and then bear right again. The way is now a stony track going uphill.

(7) A drive joins from the left but go forward and right signed 'Public Footpath'. You join a minor metalled road, go forward and right signed again 'Public Footpath'. You cross a cattle grid.

High level path near Castle Drogo

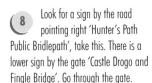

8 Look for a sign by the road pointing right 'Hunter's Path Public Bridlepath', take this. There is a lower sign by the gate 'Castle Drogo and Fingle Bridge'. Go through the gate.

Castle Drogo 1910-1930, designed by Sir Edwin Lutyens for Julius Drewe, stands prominently on the hill above.

The grassy, stoney track has a sharp right angle going left. You reach a wooden seat where there is a superb view of the wooded Teign Gorge below.

Heather

There are three somewhat different common heathers growing on Dartmoor and they all occur along a relatively short stretch of this path, mostly on the left hand-side as you travel.

The tallest and most easily distinguished is ling, *Caluna vulgaris*, a woody plant growing up to two feet tall with mostly purple flowers. Once used for primitive thatching and brooms. Widespread is bell heather *Erica cinerea* the bees first choice to make heather honey! Also present here but more sparingly is crossleaved heath *Erica tetralix*. These last two are much more similar with pinker flowers but the cross-leaved heath will thrive on the damper patches. It tends to flower at the top of each stalk whereas the bell heather flowers the whole way up the stems.

9 Ignore a footpath going left up steps signed 'Castle Drogo. The path then swings right where grows some cross-leaved heath.

An attractive flower growing by the wayside is rosebay willow herb. Its distinctive spiky vivid pink appearance makes it stand out. You will often find it in recently disturbed soil because it has very light wind-born seeds so is among the first plants to colonise a site. In fact after the London Blitz it soon provided colour on bomb sites being nicknamed 'fireweed'. It is also present in North America and is the floral emblem chosen for the Yukon.

Footpath sign along the way to Castle Drogo

Castle Drogo

The castle is the embodiment of one man's desire to reside amongst his supposed ancestors. He was Julius Drewe, an early entrepreneur in the grocery business. He ran the Home & Colonial chain of stores for eleven years and was so successful he was then able to retire, keeping his shareholding, to build his dream castle.

Julius Drewe employed the foremost architect of the day, Edwin Lutyens, and believe it or not had even greater plans than was actually built. It is interesting that despite its historic theme, for instance using weathered stone to give an impression of age, its design was progressive with dish washers, generating plant etc.

When the trees cease on the right you can look back to Chagford and Kes Tor behind it, if conditions are clear.

10 There is a second footpath going left up steps: 'Castle Drogo' again ignore. But in a couple of yards on the right is a bare rock outcrop Sharp Tor which provides a superb viewpoint.

11 The path has a little steep rocky decline but press on. Ignore a path signed left 'Drewsteignton' but go forward on the 'Hunter's Path' also signed 'Drewsteignton', underneath it says 'Fingle Bridge'.

You pass through a pair of old granite gateposts look for the slots that

Ant's nest on the descent

accommodated the wooden rails which served as a gate.

12 You come to a wooden seat 'Ronnie's Seat' and just beyond, fork right signed 'Public

Bridle Path Fingle Bridge'. It is then downhill, sometimes steeply, all the way back to the Fingle Bridge car park. Note the large untidy ants' nests on the left going down so take care if you sit to rest!